How to Build a Computer

(For Beginners)

Student Version

By John H. Gower III

Cover Created & Designed by John Gower III

ISBN-13: 978-1468097924 (Sixth Edition Paperback)

ISBN-10: 146809792X

Printed in the United States of America.

Other books with the same title by the author;

ISBN: 978-1463739799 (Fifth Edition Paperback)

ISBN: 978-1257803057 (First Edition Paperback)

ISBN: 978-1257838905 (Second Edition Paperback)

ISBN: 978-1463664060 (Fourth Edition Paperback)

Students Name: _____

Teacher: _____

Class: _____

School: _____

Table of Contents

Contents

PART III

✓ **It is Time to build!**

Contents

Introduction

Ever since the birth of computers people all around the world have wanted to get their hands on the knowledge. People spend a lot of money in colleges to get a degree with computers. However, there are people out there that do not have that opportunity.

Imagine that you do not need a degree or have to take classes to build a computer from scratch. You can learn about it as simply as reading a book and enjoying yourself.

This book provides all the details that will give you that knowledge on how to build a computer.

I am a published author trying to reach readers around the world with my new book called, "How to build a Computer (For Beginners)". John Gower III is the author, and creator of this book. Visit his website at http://www.jghitech.com for more information about him.

Part I

What You Need to Know

Chapter 1

Gathering Information

So you want to build a **Computer**? Well, first question you should ask yourself is, "what kind of performance you would like to receive out of it"? Do you want a computer that can be capable of playing games on it? Alternatively, do you want just one you can browse the **Internet** with and do word documents?

Section 1-1:

1) Write a short paragraph on what type of computer you are looking to build.

_____

_____
_____
_____
_____

When you are finish answering the question for **Section 1-1**, your first step is to gather information. What I mean by that is set your budget on how much you want to spend and compare prices.

If you do not have access to a computer that has the internet, you can go to your local library to get internet access from one of their computers free.

Go to google.com, search for parts and start comparing prices that fit your budget.

Now, I suggest that you get a paper and list the parts you will need for pricing. If you are familiar with the **AMD** or **Intel Processors**, I recommend **AMD** because I worked with it a lot and it is a good company.

On the following page, there is a list of parts you will need to start pricing.

It will take a while for you to compare prices with these parts. Just use your best judgment on buying each part. Remember, your goal is to save money.

Browse around take your time and you will get the best performance out of what you buy. Remember, that the higher the memory is the faster the computer will perform. Same with the processor speed three point five **gigahertz** is a standard good speed to go with. As for the memory, two **gigabyte(s)** of **memory** is the minimum you should purchase. Not anything lower than that is worth buying.

Write down the lists of **computer hardware** and **computer software** on a piece of paper with spaces in between. You will need them for reference back to it later on.

Computer Hardware:

- **Video Card (Graphics Card)**
- **Motherboard**
- **Processor**
- **Memory**
- **Tower Case**
- **Power Supply**
- **Hard Drive**
- **Monitor**
- **CD Rom Drive**
- **Keyboard and Mouse**
- **Floppy A: Drive (optional)**

Computer Software:

- **Microsoft Office 2007 Professional**
- **Operating System**

(Windows XP or Windows 7)

I would recommend Microsoft Windows XP for the following reason, that Windows 7 is not compatible with some older computer parts.

Section 1-2:

Questions 1-2 are multiple-choice questions for Chapter 1.

1) Which of the following is **<u>not</u>** a computer hardware part?

   a. Video Card (Graphics Card)
   b. Case
   c. Motherboard
   d. Microsoft Office 2007 Professional
   e. None of the above.

2)   What is a good site to search for computer parts?

   a. Amazon.com
   b. Google.com
   c. eBay.com
   d. pricewatch.com
   e. All of the above.

3)   Define the list of all the Computer Hardware and Software parts that are in the back of the book.

   Write them down on a piece of paper if you have not completed it already. Once finished hand them in to the teacher.

Chapter 2

Buying the Parts

The first thing you should consider doing when buying the parts, is to decide how much you are willing to spend. Now for example, my budget is $1500.

The first thing you want to do is to price motherboards. I like the **AMD** processors, so I am going to price motherboards that have the compatibility to support the processor **AMD**.

Sometimes stores carry **barebones**, which are cases with the **power supply**, and sometimes the **motherboard** is already in there.

In my example, we are going to buy a bare bone computer. I will show you some sites to check out on the next page.

You can purchase your computer parts either online or at a computer store. Here are some examples of great websites to go to;

- http://www.tigerdirect.com
- http://www.pricewatch.com

It is very important to check the **sockets (referring on the motherboard)** because there are certain sockets that can fit the processor slot. That is only if you purchase the processor separately from the motherboard.

They sometimes come in bundles so if you are new to this, I recommend that you purchase the bundle package that comes with the processor.

For example, I went to tirgerdirect.com. You want to purchase the Biostar N68S3B GeForce Barebones Kit - Biostar N68S3B Motherboard, AMD Phenom II X4 805 CPU, CPU Fan, Patriot 8GB (2x 4GB) DDR3 RAM, Seagate 1TB HDD, 22x DVDRW, Thermal take ATX Mid-Tower, 450-Watt PSU for $299.99. This comes with the case motherboard, processor and fan, memory, CD Rom drive and hard drive.

Barebones Example:

The Barebones Example above contains the case the memory, processor, hard drive, CD Rom drive and motherboard all included.

You need to get the keyboard, monitor, operating system (Windows 7), and mouse.

Next purchase the monitor for $79.99. The, I-Inc iP-192ABB 19" Class Widescreen LCD Monitor.
The I-Inc iP-192ABB 19" Class Widescreen LCD Monitor delivers a crisp and pristine quality picture, with 1440 x 900 pixels at a 16:10 aspect ratio. With 16.7 million colors and 5ms response time, the I-Inc iP-192ABB 19" Class Widescreen LCD Monitor not only makes your images pop, it makes them come alive on screen. Combine these traits with low energy consumption and the I-Inc iP-192ABB 19" Class Widescreen LCD Monitor sounds like the ideal match for your personal computer.

In **Example 1-1** below shows a picture of a 19" LCD Monitor.

Example 1-1: 19" LCD Monitor:

Now you will need to purchase the operating system. You want to get **Windows 7** for it. Therefore, I am going to go to tigerdirect.com and type in the search Windows 7. I am going to purchase Microsoft Windows 7 Home Premium Operating System Software DVD for $99.99 on tigerdirect.com.

With Microsoft Windows 7 Home Premium Operating System Software, you will get the best entertainment experience on your PC!

Windows 7 Home Premium makes it easy to create a home network and share all of your favorite photos, videos, and music.

You can even watch, pause, and rewind TV or record it to watch whenever and wherever you want. For the best entertainment experience on your PC, choose Windows 7 Home Premium.

Next, you will want to purchase the mouse and keyboard. I will go to tirgerdirect.com and type in the search box, keyboard and mouse combo. I want to purchase the Logitech 920-002565 MK120 Keyboard and Mouse Combo - USB, Optical Mouse, 1000 DPI, Spill Resistant Design, and Black for $19.99.

In the picture above are the Logitech 920-002565 MK120 Keyboard and Mouse Combo - USB, Optical Mouse, 1000 DPI, Spill Resistant Design, black.

Ok, now once you have priced all the **hardware** and **software** that you need to build a computer, it does not have to be exactly the one I am building. This is only an example. You can purchase them online, or at a computer store near you. Then move on to part II once you have received all of your necessary computer parts.

Part II

Learn How to Prepare Yourself.

© by John Gower III

Chapter 3

Getting the Right Tools Ready to Build

Now you need to get the tools ready to build. You can purchase a tool kit online or at a store like Staples or Office Max. That has all the tools you will need for building your PC. They are very inexpensive to buy, because they come in handy when you are building your **Computer**. **IT Professionals** always carry these tools.

All tools are fully **demagnetized** to protect your computer's hard drive or magnetic media from damage. Each tool is conveniently stored in a custom designed case, an the tools tackle minor electronic maintenance jobs with ease. View example 1-1 on the following page.

Example 1-1:

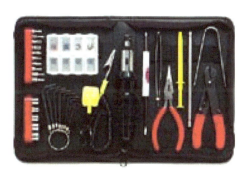

In example, 1-1 shows a picture of the Belkin Professional Computer Service Tool Kit.

What you need is a Phillips screwdriver and an **ESD** static band to ground to help protect your valuable computer equipment from dangerous static electricity. That should wrap up all you should need to know before you start building your computer.

Please answer the following questions are on page 28-29. Once finished please hand in your work to your teacher to grade.

Section 1-1:

1) What does ESD stand for and why is it important to have one on while you work on your computer?

_____

_____

_____

_____

_____

_____

2) Explain the difference between demagnetized tools and magnetized tools.

_____

_____

_____

_____

_____

_____

_____

_____

_____

3)   What happens if you do not use an ESD?

_____

_____

_____

_____

_____

_____

_____

_____

_____

Chapter 4

Preparing Your Workspace

Selecting the proper workspace for your computer-building project is very important. You need enough space to layout all of your parts, and you need good lighting to see what you are doing inside the case.

A large computer desk is a good area to work on, where you can have the parts all to one side. Another choice is a large kitchen table with overhead lights.

You will want to avoid working on the ground, and especially the carpet because of the threat of static electricity.

You will need to have an **ESD** Wrist Strap handy. Use it at all times when handling your PC parts and building your computer.

Once you have selected your workspace, go ahead and layout all of your tools and parts. Now we are ready to get started building the PC!

Section 1-1:

1) Why is it important to prepare your workspace?

_____

_____

_____

_____

_____

_____

_____

Part III

It is Time to Build!

Chapter 5

Building Step's

Now that we have our workspace ready to go with our parts and tools laid out, we need to get our case ready to install everything.

Most cases are laid out generally the same way, but our example assumes that you are using a standard sized **ATX** type case. Some cases have a removable tray that the motherboard fits on also, but the holes to install the motherboard will be the same. If these directions do not match the type of case that you have, make sure to consult the documentation that came with your case.

Section 1-1:

1) What is the difference between an ATX computer case and an AT computer case?

    _____

    _____

    _____

    _____

    _____

    _____

Please read the following steps <u>carefully.</u>

Step 1- Opening the Case

Example 1-1:

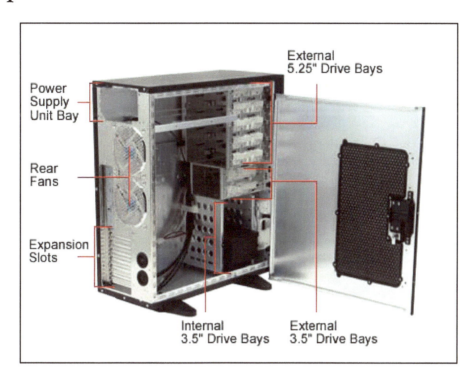

In the example 1-1, shows an example of what the side of computer case appears like.

Open the left side of the case by removing the two screws in the back that hold the side on. Once the screws are removed, you may need to slide the panel back completely along the rails to remove it. Your case may have clips instead of screws, and you will need to undo the clips to remove the side. If you have a more expensive case that is locking, make sure the lock is undone before trying to remove the side of the case.

Once you have access to the inside of the case, you will probably see some hardware that has been included, including instructions. You may want to go ahead and open the bag of hardware and have the instructions handy as you follow along.

Example 1-2:

In example, 1-2, shows what the front of the computer case appears like.

Now is probably the best time to get your wrist strap out and get yourself properly grounded to avoid damage to your parts as we start working. Follow the installation directions of your wrist strap and continue below. If you choose to work without a wrist strap, make sure to touch the case every time you start working on the computer, to remove static electricity from your body.

Step 2- Understanding the Inside of the Case

After looking inside the case for the first time, you should see many wires running in many directions. The twisted looking wires are used to connect such things as your case speaker, hard drive light, power light, and power switch. There may be an extra set of wires running from the top or the bottom of the case as well that connect to the USB ports on the front of your case if it so equipped.

You may have a fan at the bottom front of the case with a power wire running from it, which is used for cooling and airflow. There should be a speaker mounted somewhere on the front part of the case, with a wire coming from it that will later be attached to the motherboard.

If you bought a case that already has a power supply installed, you will see the power supply mounted in the upper rear, with many different power connectors coming out of it. These various connectors are used to supply power to your hard drive, CD/ROM and DVD drives, floppy drive, speaker, etc.

You will not be doing anything with these wires until you get the motherboard installed. Next move everything aside as good as you can, to make a clear open space to mount the motherboard into the case.

Step 3- Install Motherboard Standoffs

Example 1-3:

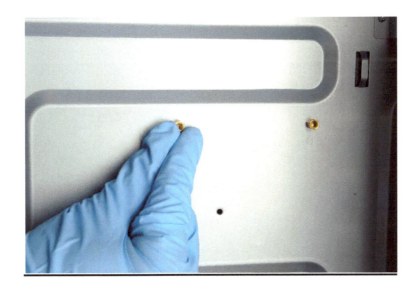

In example, 1-3 shows an illustration of installing the standoffs

Now you will want to get that bag of hardware back out that came with your case, and remove the motherboard standoffs. You will probably also need to get your needle nose pliers ready for screwing them in. The motherboard standoffs are the small screws that have a male and female end to them. This will allow a base for your motherboard to set on, that you can then attach the screws to.

Remove your motherboard from the case and packaging and examine the holes that are present on the motherboard. This is where the screws will go.

Examine the holes inside the case, hold the motherboard inside the case, and figure out where you need to screw the standoffs into the case to match the holes on the motherboard. When you think you have them all in correctly, set the motherboard on top of the standoffs one last time to make sure you did not miss any.

Make sure that you get the standoffs screwed in tightly, as these will serve as the base and support for your motherboard on the case. You can now remove the motherboard, set it aside, and continue.

Step 4- Install I/O Plate

Example 1-4:

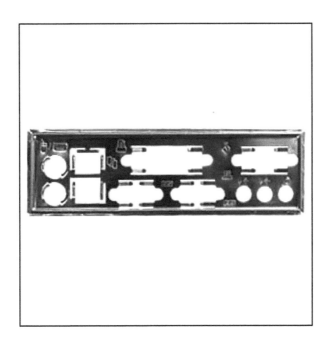

The example 1-4 shows an illustration of what an **I/O plate** appears like.

The **I/O plate** is the metallic looking piece that fits in the large rectangular space on the back of the case. It should snap into the space with ease, and will fit around all of the **I/O ports** on the back of the **motherboard** when it is installed.

Step 5- Remove front Covers on Case

Example 1-5:

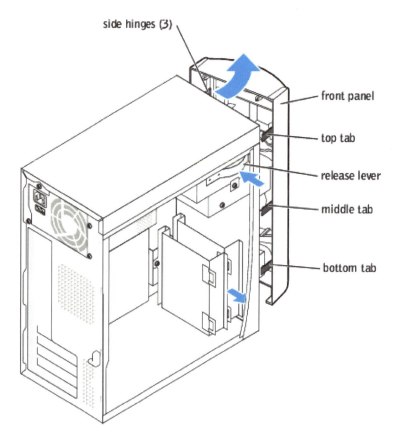

In example, 1-5 shows an illustration of how to remove the front cover of the computer case.

Now would be a good time to figure out to think about where you want to install your **DVD/CD Rom drive** and **floppy drive**.

On the front of the case, you will see the individual panels that can be removed. Depending on the size of your case, you should have a few of the larger panels towards the top. Think about where you want the **DVD/CD Rom** to be installed, and pop out that section. For aesthetics, the top most slots generally work the best.

Repeat this process for the **floppy drive** if you bought one, and remove the smaller panel below where you want your floppy drive to sit at.

NOTE: You may need to use your flat head screwdriver to gently pry the panels loose. Do not put too much effort into it though, as they should easily come out.

When it comes time to install these drives, you will now be able to slide them in from the front of the case.

We have successfully prepared the case for installing parts, and now it is time to move on and install the power supply if your case did not come with one already.

If the case that you bought already has a **power supply** installed, then you can skip this step. If not continue below.

Example 1-6:

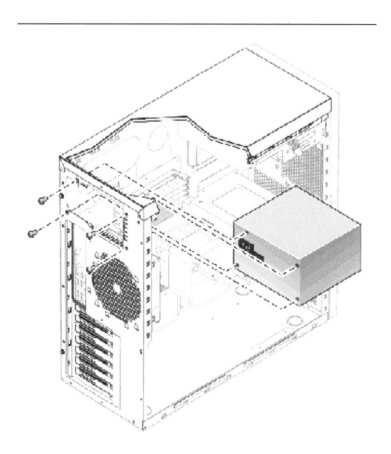

In example, 1-6 shows an illustration on how to install the power supply.

Take the power supply out of the box and make sure to switch to 115v if it is not already (If you are outside the United States, this will be different)

Mount the power supply to the upper back part of the case by inserting the **power supply** through the side of the case, and then sliding it on the support rails in the back.

NOTE: **If your power supply has two fans, make sure the second fan is pointing down.**

If you have everything lined up correctly, you should be able to attach the power supply to the case with the four screws in the back that hold it in place.

We now have the power source necessary to run everything!

The next step is to prepare the motherboard for installation. It may not even be necessary to do anything on this step, depending on the age and type of your motherboard.

Motherboards over time have lost many of the 'jumper(s)' that were required for configuring the board. Most of the setup is done with the **BIOS, (Basic Input Output System),** that are accessible when you first turn on your computer.

You will need to view your motherboard instruction manual, and see if any jumpers need to be set on the motherboard itself for configuration. Common settings include **CPU voltage** and **bus speed**, so read the directions and make sure that these or nothing else needs to be configured on motherboard before continuing.

After you set anything on the motherboard that is necessary, you will want to lay out the number of screws you need to install the motherboard inside the case. You should set the motherboard on a flat surface so you can install the CPU and memory. It is a good idea to keep the motherboard on the anti static bag that it came with, to reduce the possibility of damage due to static.

I also recommend having the motherboard manual handy as we start to build your computer. Let us now move on to installing the CPU and heat sink!

Step 6- Inspect the CPU

Example 1-7:

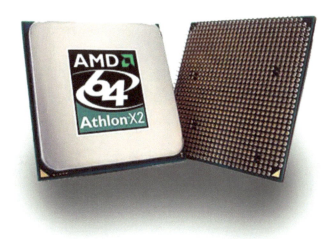

In example, 1-7 shows a picture of what the CPU will appear like.

First, before installing the CPU, we recommend that you take it out of the packaging and verify that you have received the correct one that you ordered. With all of the different core types and speeds, it is necessary to check before installing. You also want to check the pins on the underside of the processor, and make sure that all are straight with no damage. Try to avoid touching the pins with your bare fingers if possible. If everything looks good, continue.

Section 1-2:

1) Explain why is it important to make sure that you inspect the CPU before installing.

_____

_____

_____

_____

_____

_____

_____

_____

_____

Step 7- CPU Installation

Example 1-8:

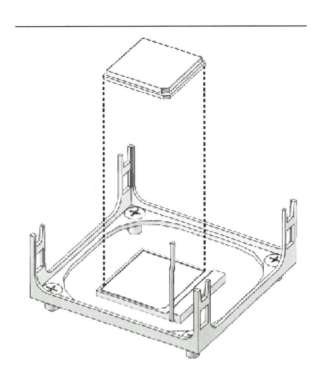

In example, 1-8 shows an illustration on installing the CPU.

Depending on your choice of **Intel** or **AMD**, your socket type may look different. Generally, all sockets on a motherboard have a latching feature, which holds the **CPU** in place.

NOTE: If these instructions do not match, your motherboard and **CPU** type, then consult the directions that came with your **CPU** for proper installation.

Unlatch the socket on the motherboard by pulling the lever up.

You should see a small triangle on one corner of the socket. You will need to match this up to the triangle on the processor, so that the triangles are oriented and in the same position. Once you have these lined up, simply set the CPU onto the socket and gently move until it falls into place.

Note: (You should not have to force the CPU in the socket. If it is not going in easily, something is wrong. Check the pins for damage if it is not sliding in correctly)

Push the lever back down to secure the **CPU** into the **socket**.

Section 1-3:

1) Explain why it is important not force the CPU in the CPU Slot.

_____

_____

_____

_____

_____

_____

_____

_____

_____

_____

_____

_____

_____

_____

_____

Step 8- Heat sink/Fan Installation

Example 1-9:

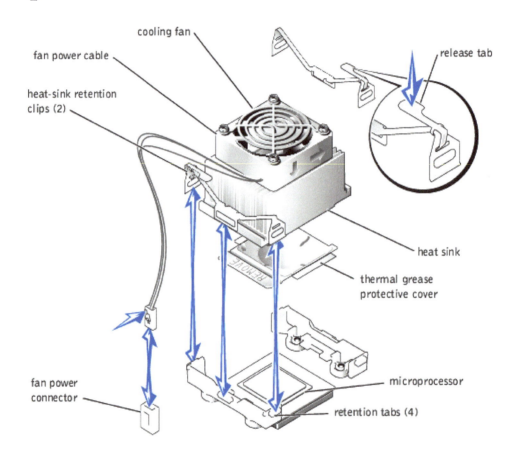

In example, 1-9 is an illustration of installing the Heat Sink/Fan.

Processors run very hot, and it is necessary to attach a cooling device to control the temperature as your computer runs. If you bought the retail version of your CPU selection, as we recommended, it should have come with a fan and heat sink combo.

Again, depending on your choice between **AMD** and Intel, your heat sink and fan may look different. I recommend following the directions that came with your **CPU** for specifics on attaching to the top of the **CPU**, but here are the general directions.

Remove the heat sink/fan from the box, and make sure to remove the plastic cover that is over the bottom. This plastic cover is to keep the **thermal grease** in place with shipment. You need to remove the plastic cover so that the thermal grease can attach to the CPU and improve heat transfer.

Place the heat sink and fan combo squarely on the **CPU**. Attach the mounting brackets from the heat sink over the tabbed parts of your **CPU socket**. Many times this is a small square tab sticking out on each side of the socket. It will probably be necessary to use a flat screwdriver to push down when attaching the second side.

There may be a large lever that you need to turn clockwise and push down to finish attaching the heat sink. This insures the heat sink and fan are firmly attached.

Section 1-4:

1) Why is it important to put thermal grease between the heat sink and the CPU?

_____

_____

_____

_____

_____

_____

_____

_____

_____

_____

_____

Step 9- Connect CPU Fan to Motherboard

Example 1-10:

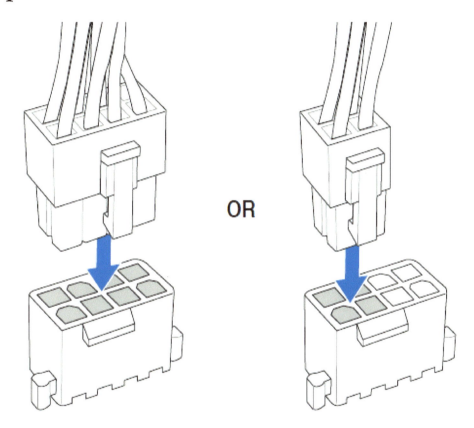

In example, 1-10 shows an illustration of connecting the CPU Fan to the Motherboard.

Your motherboard should have a place to connect the wire from the CPU fan to, and it should match the number of pins that the connector has. Please consult your motherboard manual to see where you need to connect your CPU fan to for power. This is an important step, because you do not want to run the computer without proper cooling to the CPU, as it may cause damage.

You have just installed the Processor and are ready to continue, building your new computer. The next step in the building process is memory installation.

Step 10- Memory installation

Example 1-11:

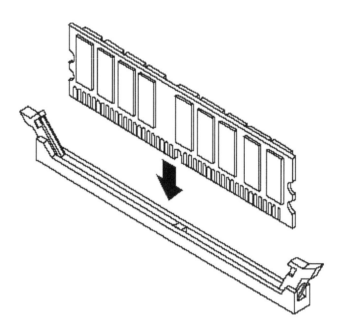

In example, 1-11 shows an illustration of a memory stick being, installed on a motherboard.

The next step is to get the memory installed and this is a very easy step.

1. Remove the memory from the packaging and notice the number of pins on the bottom of the memory module. One side will have more pins than the other side, and there will be a large gap in between the two sides of pins.

2. Look at the memory slots on the motherboard and you can see the same pattern, with one side having more pins than the other does.

3. Make sure that you match the pattern up on both the memory stick and the motherboard. Place the memory into the slot, and firmly push down.

4. The memory should 'snap' into place, and you will want to make sure that the plastic tabs at each end of the memory slot are tightly secure to the sides of the memory.

5. If you have more than one memory module, repeat the above process to install the remainder of the memory.

NOTE: You should not have to really force the memory into the slot, it should go fairly easily. Make sure you have the memory turned the right way, and that the side tabs are not in your way as you push it into the slot.

Now that we have the 'core' of our components installed on the motherboard, it is time to install the motherboard itself.

You have installed the CPU and memory before installing the motherboard because it is generally easier to work with the motherboard out of the case. You can however, install these items while the motherboard was in the case.

Since you have already prepared the case, installing the motherboard into the case should be easy.

Section 1-5:

1)   Explain why it is important not force the memory stick when installing it in the memory slot on the motherboard.

_____

_____

_____

_____

_____

_____

_____

_____

_____

_____

_____

_____

_____

_____

_____

_____

Step 11- Mount the Motherboard onto the Standoffs

Example 1-12:

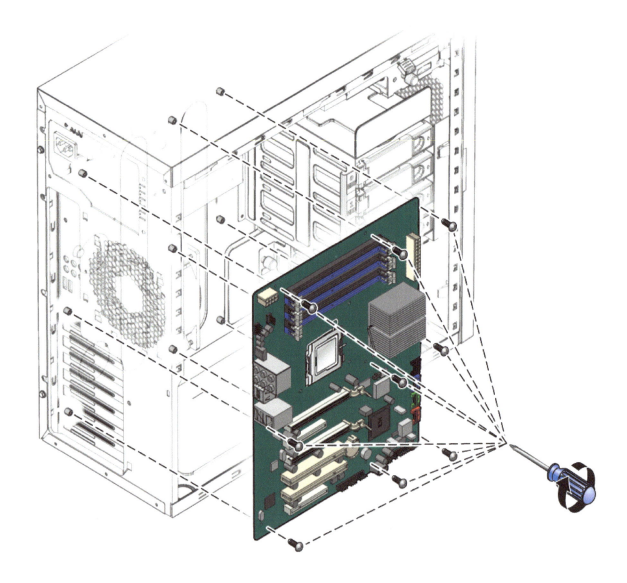

In example, 1-12 shows an illustration of how to mount the motherboard onto the standoffs.

1. Put the motherboard into the case, and set it onto the open screw holes, which have been created by the standoffs. If you matched the pattern before to the case, you should have the same number of openings to insert screws into.

   (To get the holes to line up perfectly, you may need to push the motherboard back towards where the **I/O plate** is, as this generally fits snugly)

2. Insert screws into all of the holes and tighten gently. It is not necessary to over tighten these screws.

You should now be looking at your motherboard installed inside the case! The **I/O ports** should be sticking out the back and should fit squarely and snug. If you could not install all of the screws or the **I/O ports** do not fit correctly through the plate, make sure to correct this before you continue. Ensure that the slots on the motherboard line up correctly and are straight to add on cards to be easily installed.

You have the motherboard installed, and now it is time to get all of the cables on the inside connected.

With the motherboard installed, it is time to connect the internal cables that run from the case.

Step 12- Connect the Cables from the Case

Example 1-13

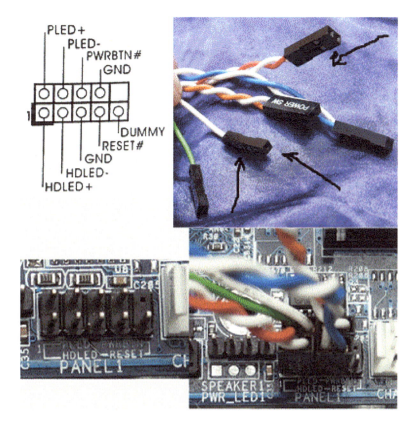

In example, 1-13 shows an illustration on how to install the cables from the computer case.

It is difficult to give detailed instructions for this, because every motherboard and case is different. In general, you should have twisted cables for the speaker, case fan, and hard drive light, power light, power switch and reset buttons. You may also have cables for **USB port(s)** if your case has them built in.

Your motherboard manual will have a detailed diagram on where to attach these. Follow the directions on where these go for a smooth installation. Make sure to attach the wires in the correct orientation, usually each set of wires has a ground so it is easy to figure out which way they go.

If you are not using onboard video via the motherboard, then the next step is to install the video card into the proper slot.

If you bought the **video card** separately and plan to install a separate video card for your new computer, please continue the step. If you bought a motherboard that has onboard video built in, you may skip this step.

Remove the card from the original packaging and look at the slot type on the card. It should match the slot that is on your motherboard. (**AGP** and **PCI** Express are currently the most popular video card types)

Hold the card in the proximity of where it will be installed in the slot. You will need to remove the back cover plate with your screwdriver where the card will stick through the back of the case.

Gently install the card into the slot, by pushing until it fits snug into place. There may be an extra tab as part of the slot that wraps around and helps secure the card.

Replace the screw that you removed for the slot, to secure the card to the back of the case.

That is it for the video card installation, not too difficult is it. Next, we need to attach the power supply connector(s) to our motherboard. In This Case, we are going to use the on board **AGP**.

This is a very quick step, and will allow us to prepare ourselves for a test to see how smoothly our computer-building project is going.

Step 13- Attach the Power Supply Connector

Example 1-14:

 In example, 1-14 shows an illustration of the power supply cord connected to the motherboard.

 If you have an **ATX style power supply**, it will have one large connector, and possibly a smaller square connector that both need to be attached to provide power to the motherboard. They can only be attached one way, and each have a tab that needs to be pressed as you push them into their respective slots. You should here a 'click' and be able to feel when they are secure.

With the CPU, memory, and video card installed on the motherboard, and our case cables and power supply connected. Now is a good time to do a quick power up test to see if we get video or not. To make sure that the fans are all operating correctly.

1. Plug in your power strip to the wall and turn it on. Then plug the PC power cable that came with your motherboard or power supply, from the surge strip to the back of the power supply. Make sure that the power supply is set to the proper voltage (115v in the US) and that the switch is in the on position.

A small LED light may come on somewhere on the motherboard, telling you that the motherboard now has power. Your motherboard may or may not have such a light.

2. Plug the monitor and keyboard into their respective ports.

3. Make sure that your monitor also is plugged into your power strip.

NOTE: Make sure you have the CPU fan connected to the proper place on the motherboard for power. Starting the computer without proper CPU cooling, can cause damage to the processor, even if it does not run for very long.

Now comes the moment of truth. Go ahead and push the power button on the front of the case (it should be the largest button on the front) and see what happens.

If all is well, you should hear the power supply fan, CPU fan and case fan(s) start, and see some video on the monitor for the first time. Here you want to make sure that all fans are operating as they should, and that you have video. If you can see something on the monitor, then it is very likely that the CPU and memory are operating properly and that everything is installed properly.

If everything that was just mentioned happens, then shut off the computer and move on to the next step.

Step 14- Oh No, Nothing is Happening!

If the computer will not power on, then double check your power connections from the power supply to the motherboard and try again. Double check to make sure your power switch cable is installed correctly to the motherboard.

If you fail to see video, then make sure your monitor is attached correctly. If you hear the fans starting but do not see any video, make sure that you have attached the second power connector from your power supply to the motherboard. It should be a smaller type connector.

If you are still having problems, reverse your steps and reinstall the memory and video card and CPU. If you cannot get the machine to power on at this point, and are sure everything is installed correctly, then it is likely that you have a defective component. You will know if the power supply is defective, because the fan will not run when you power it on. Consult with whom you bought your parts from, for more assistance on troubleshooting and determining which part is defective.

The next step on how to build a computer is to install the hard drive. Now that you know your main components are working after doing our quick power up test, you can now finish building the computer. You are going to configure all of the drives, and install them in the case.

Step 15- Installing the Hard Drive

Example 1-15

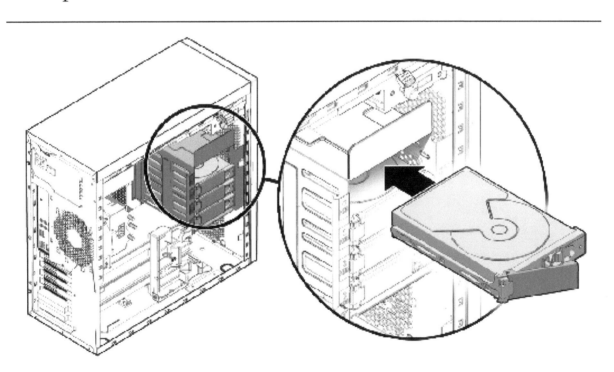

Example 1-15 shows an illustration of a hard drive being installed in a computer case.

1) Remove the hard drive from its packaging/anti static bag.
2) Select where you want to place the hard drive within the case, usually there are a couple of spots labeled **'HDD'** where the hard drive is intended to go.
3) On the top of the hard drive, there should be a diagram telling you how to jumper the drive for installation.

If this is your only hard drive, and it is an **SATA** type drive, then you can set the drive as 'master'. Follow the diagram and place the jumper across the pins to make this setting. Many times leaving a **jumper** off completely, will default the drive as master.

4) If you are installing an **IDE** type drive with another IDE hard drive or DVD/CD-ROM drive on the same cable, then set your jumper for **master** or **cable select**. **Cable Select** means the computer will auto configure it for you. If you do set the drive to master, make sure that you set the other drive you are installing on the same cable to 'slave' by setting the **jumper** correctly.

5)   Once you have the drive jumper and setup correctly, push it into the slot you want and line up the screw holes with the case. Make sure to leave the back to attach the connections open, you will want this facing to the rear.

6)   Attach the four screws to the case and you are set!

You are now onto installing the hard **CD ROM** drives.

When you prepared the case before, I recommended that you remove the front cover(s) for the location where you wanted to install your CD-Rom and/or DVD drive.

The next step is to make sure they are configured correctly, and position them in the case.

Remove the drive from its packaging/anti static bag.

Your drive should be an **IDE** type drive, and you will need to configure the drive, depending on if it is installed on its own cable or not. If the drive is on its own cable, and you have already installed an **SATA** hard drive, then set the jumper to master on the drive. Like the hard drive that you configured before, there should be a diagram somewhere on the drive, or labeled on the drive directly on how to configure it as master. If the drive is sharing a cable with the hard drive, I recommend setting it as cable select, if your **IDE hard drive** was set to **cable select**, or slave if the **IDE hard drive** has been set to master.

You should have already removed the front cover of where you want it to go so slide the drive into the case from the front.

Line up the holes with the drive and the case, and make sure that the drive is flush with the front edge of the case.

Attach the screws to the case to secure the drive.

If you have more than one CD-Rom or DVD drive to install, repeat the exact same process as above.

Now that you have all of your drives secure in the case, it is time to hook everything up.

This is starting to look like a real computer is not it. You are approaching the home stretch so hang in there. You need to attach the drives to your motherboard and power supply next. The cables you need to attach everything, to should have come with either your motherboard or individual drives. Depending on if you bought the retail or OEM versions. Get the cables out, as you will need them to install the drives.

Step 16- Connect Hard Drive Cables

Example 1-16

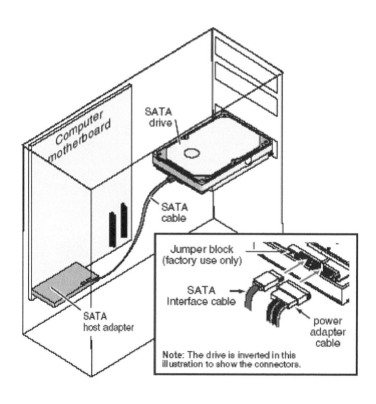

In example, 1-16 shows an illustration of a SATA hard drive being installed in a computer case.

If you bought an **SATA hard drive**, the cable going from the drive to the motherboard is very easy to install, as the connectors can only fit one way into the drive and motherboard connections.

Example 1-17:

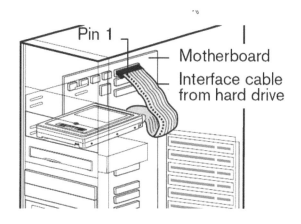

In example, 1-17 shows an illustration of an **IDE cable** being connected from the hard drive to the motherboard.

Connect one end to the hard drive, and the other connector to the hard drive, aligning the connectors properly. If you bought an IDE hard drive, more than likely the connectors are tabbed and can only fit one way into the connection slots. To be sure, when connecting the **IDE cable** to the hard drive, you want the red stripe facing closest to the power connecter.

This is also known as **'pin 1'**, and is always installed this way. Attach the other end of the cable to the motherboard by installing it into the slot. Make sure both connections are snug and tight.

Attach the **SATA** power connector from the power supply to the back of the hard drive if you have this drive type or one of the standard power connectors if you have an IDE version.

(A standard power connector will be the same shape as the connection slot on your drive, long and rectangular).

Step 17- Connect CD-Rom / DVD Drive Cables

Example 1-19:

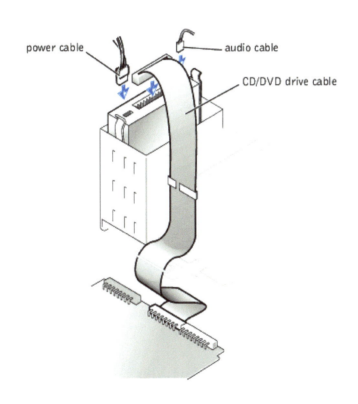

In example, 1-17 shows an illustration of a CD-ROM drive being connected to a motherboard.

As previously described in this chapter, related to an **IDE cable** more than likely the connectors are tabbed, and can only fit one way into the connection slots. To be sure when connecting the **IDE cable** to the hard drive, you want the red stripe facing closest to the power connecter. This is also known as '**pin 1**', and is always installed this way. Attach the other end of the cable to the motherboard by installing it into the slot. Ensure that both connections are snug and tight.

Attach a standard power connector from the power supply to the back of the drive. (A standard power connector will be the same shape as the connection slot on your drive, long and rectangular).

All of your drives are now secure, connected and have a power source. You can now finish connecting things to the outside of the case.

Now that everything is finished up on the inside of the machine, you need to connect all of our external devices such as the keyboard, mouse, and monitor.

If you still have, the monitor connected from before on our quick power up test great! If not, go ahead and connect it to the video port on the video card now. If you have onboard video, this will be mixed in with the other **I/O ports** on the back of the case. If you installed it separately to a slot, it will be farther down in the back.

Connect the keyboard, mouse, and speakers to the matching **I/O ports** on the back of the case. Many times these are color coded so it makes it easier to connect. They are also labeled next to the ports with a mouse symbol for mouse, keyboard for keyboard etc.

Depending on how you plan on connecting to the internet, either connect the phone line to your modem OR connect the network cable that runs from you cable modem, DSL modem, or wireless router to the network port on the back of your computer. It will be the port that looks similar to a phone jack, just slightly larger.

If you bought a scanner or printer, you can go ahead and connect it now. Windows will detect and set the drivers for you when you run installation for the first time.

With everything attached to the inside and the outside of your new computer, you are now ready to try and do a full boot test for the first time. Keep the side off the case to ensure you can make sure everything is functioning properly, and troubleshoot if necessary. Now you are almost finished!

Chapter 6

Running the Computer

The goal of the first boot is to test out all of your hardware and make sure that there are no problems before you prepare to install the operating system.

Now that everything is connected, go ahead and press the power button to start the machine up. Check and make sure that things are operating like on our previous quick power on test, mainly that the fans are working and we have video.

If the computer has been built correctly to this point, you should see a posting of the memory available and then a message stating that a first boot device or OS needs to be installed. Since you have nothing on the new hard drive, this is normal, and shows that the computer is properly seeing the hard drive.

Next, you need to go into the **BIOS** and configure the **DVD drive** to be bootable for installation of **Windows**.

You will need to access the BIOS now on your computer, and this is usually accomplished by pressing and holding down the 'delete' key after you turn on your computer. Depending on your **BIOS** type, the key or keys you enter may be different. Please consult your motherboard manual on how to access the **BIOS** if it is not the delete key.

You will also need to follow the instructions in your motherboard manual for changing the first boot up device, and you need to set the first boot device to be your DVD drive.

Why, you may ask, do you need to change the computer to boot from the DVD drive?

The newest versions of Windows are on media that is bootable, and will start the installation process on their own when you turn on the computer. When you have a hard drive with nothing on it, this is a quick and easy way to get your operating system installed.

You should not be too concerned with any of the other settings in the **BIOS** at this time. Later, after you have everything installed and working properly, you can come back to the **BIOS** to tweak some settings, but for now it is not necessary.

Let's get ready to install our operating system on the hard drive.

This step may not even be necessary, but I wanted to include it for reference. The newest versions of Windows, including Windows XP and Windows Vista, have a way to partition and format the hard drive during the installation process. If you plan to install either of these versions of Windows on a new hard drive as a standard installation, then you do not have to do anything except specify how you want the drive to setup during the install process. Skip the information below and continue on to the next step.

If you plan to install multiple operating systems, or want the drive to split up into separate sections or partitions, then you may want to do this before starting the install. Third party utilities are available to handle partitioning and formatting, some of which are free.

This will need to be finished to the hard drive prior to installing windows if you have a specific way you want to set the drive up. Make sure to use a compatible file type if you do your own partitioning. **NTFS** for Windows XP is recommended, Windows Vista use a newer version of **NTFS.** Ensure that your partition utility program will set the drive up to be ready for Vista if you are planning to install it.

You are going to assume that this is a standard Windows installation, and continue on to the next step. With your new installation of Windows, you have now completed building your first computer, and you are ready to start tweaking your system!

You have now just built your first computer!

Congratulations!

Chapter 7

Finalization

Now boot your computer up. Follow the steps that Windows asks you when you boot into windows. Now if you do not have internet, call your local phone or cable company and purchase an internet package deal.

Schedule for them to come out to hook the internet up, and connect your cable from the modem to the new computer you built.

Now once you have the internet working correctly. Go to the start button on the computer, and search for the Windows Update button; it should be in the programs tab. Run the Windows Updates. Follow each step, let it run, and restart automatically. Now you can enjoy your newly built computer.

Let us see how much you have learned!

I will give you a list of questions about what you have learned in this book. Questions start on page 89.

Please use a Number 2 pencil. Section 1 questions 1 thru 5 will be multiple-choice questions. Section 2 questions 6 thru 7 will be essay questions. Section 3 questions 8 thru 10 will be also multiple-choice questions. Good Luck!

Name: _____   Date: _____

FINAL TEST

Section 1:

Questions 1 thru 5 will be Multiple Choice.

1. Which of the following is **not** a computer part you will need to assemble your PC?

    a. Motherboard
    b. Processor
    c. Operating System
    d. BIOS

2. Which of the following is <u>not</u> an Operating System?

    a. Windows XP
    b. Windows 7
    c. MS DOS
    d. Windows 300

3. What tool protects you from static electricity while you are working on building your computer?

    a. Duct Tape
    b. Static Tape
    c. Electrical Tape
    d. Static Wrist Band

4. What is the best area for you to work?

    a. A large computer desk
    b. On the Floor
    c. Outside on the grass
    d. None of the above.

5. Once you have selected your workspace you must then_____.

   a. Buy another part
   b. Layout your parts
   c. Put on you ESD
   d. None of the above

Section 2:

Questions 6 and 7 are essay questions. Please write at least two paragraphs per essay.

6. Why is it important to be careful and follow each step carefully while building a computer?

Write at least one paragraph for this question.

_____
_____
_____
_____
_____
_____

_____

_____

_____

_____

_____

_____

_____

_____

_____

_____

_____

_____

_____

_____

_____

_____

_____

_____

7.   Why is it important to wear an ESD wrist strap?

Write at least two paragraphs for this question.

_____

_____

_____

_____

Section 3:

Questions 8 thru 10 are multiple choices.

8.   What is the first step in the building process?

a.   Install Motherboard standoffs
b.   Inspect the CPU
c.   Open the Left Side of the Case
d.   None of the Above

9.   What is the proper voltage that the power supply should be set for?

a. 225v
b. 360v
c. 115v
d. None of the above

10. What should you do when the power does not go on when you hit the power button?

   a. Trash it
   b. Find someone to help you
   c. Check you power connections
   d. None of the above

11. Explain why it is important **not** to force a CPU chip in the CPU Slot.

_____

_____

_____

_____

_____

_____

12. Explain what a graphics card does.

_____

_____

_____

_____

_____

_____

_____

13. What is thermal grease?

     _____

     _____

     _____

     _____

     _____

     _____

     _____

14. What is thermal grease used for?

_____

_____

_____

_____

_____

_____

_____

_____

15. Explain the difference between a SATA and IDE hard drive.

_____

_____

_____

_____

_____

_____

_____

_____

_____

_____

_____

_____

_____

_____

16. Define gigahertz.

_____

_____

_____

_____

_____

_____

_____

_____

_____

_____

_____

17. What does BIOS stand for and what key do you press to go into the BIOS?

_____

_____

_____

_____

_____

_____

_____

18. Define AGP.

_____

_____

_____

_____

_____

_____

_____

19. Define PCI.

_____

_____

_____

_____

_____

_____

_____

_____

_____

20. What are I/O ports?

_____

_____

_____

_____

_____

_____

_____

_____

21. What is an I/O shield?

_____

_____

_____

_____

_____

_____

_____

_____

22. What is the difference between an I/O shield and
I/O ports?

_____

_____

_____

_____

_____

_____

_____

_____

_____

_____

_____

_____

_____

_____

_____

_____

_____

_____

_____

_____

_____

_____

_____

_____

Once you are finished, please give the book to your teacher.

Certificate of Excellence

In recognition of the commitment to achieve
Professional excellence, this certifies that

_____

Has successfully completed the course of

HOW TO BUILD A COMPUTER (FOR BEGINNERS)

Conducted from_____ to_____

At my company

His/her performance was grade_____

Given under the seal of university

Head of the deptt.   *Teacher*

Course contents

FUNDAMENTALS   *COMPUTER HARDWARE&*
COMPUTER & TECHNOLOGY   *SOFTWARE*

Glossary

Glossary

A

AGP (**A**ccelerated **G**raphics **P**ort) A high-speed 32-bit port from Intel for attaching a display adapter to a PC. It provides a direct connection between the card and memory, and only one AGP slot is on the motherboard. AGP was introduced as a higher-speed alternative to PCI display adapters, and it freed a PCI slot for another peripheral device. The brown AGP slot is slightly shorter than the white PCI slot and is located about an inch farther back. AGP was superseded by PCI Express. *(Refer to Page 63, Chapter 5)*

AMD Short for *Advanced Micro Devices,* a manufacturer of chips for personal computers. AMD is challenging Intel with a set of Intel-compatible microprocessors. *(Refer to Page 14, Chapter 2)*

ATX Advanced Technology Extended (ATX) is a motherboard form factors used for PC systems. *(Refer to Page 32, Chapter 5)*

ATX Style power supply A power supply designed specifically for an ATX style computer case. *(Refer to Page 65, Chapter 5)*

106

B

BIOS **B**asic **I**nput/**O**utput **S**ystem (BIOS), also known as the System BIOS or ROM BIOS. *(Refer to Page 43, Chapter 5)*

Bus Speed A measurement, usually in MHz, of how many times data can be transferred over the bus per second. *(Refer to Page 44, Chapter 5)*

C

Cable Select This is Plug-and-Play ATA. You plug in your ATA/IDE hard drives, set them to CSEL (Cable Select), and they determine whether they are master or slave automatically, saving you from manual configuration. *(Refer to Page 70, Chapter 5)*

CD Rom Drive (**"C**ompact **D**isc **R**ead-**o**nly **m**emory") is a pre-pressed compact disc that contains data accessible to, but not writable by, a computer for data storage and music playback. *(Refer to Page 11, Chapter 1)*

Computer Also called processor. An electronic device designed to accept data, perform prescribed mathematical and logical operations at high speed, and display the results of these operations. Compare analog computer, digital computer. *(Refer to Page 9, Chapter 1)*

Computer Hardware   The mechanical, magnetic, electronic, and electrical components that make up the computer system. *(Refer to Page 11, Chapter 1)*

Computer Software   Written programs or procedures or rules and associated documentation pertaining to the operation of a computer system and that are stored in read/write memory. *(Refer to Page 12, Chapter 1)*

CPU Socket   A CPU socket or CPU slot is a mechanical component that provides mechanical and electrical connections between a microprocessor and a printed circuit board (PCB). This allows the CPU to be replaced without soldering. *(Refer to Page 51, Chapter 5)*

CPU Voltage   Is the power supply voltage supplied to the CPU (which is a digital circuit), GPU, or other device containing a processing core. The amount of power a CPU uses, and thus the amount of heat it dissipates, is the product of this voltage and the current it draws. In modern CPUs, which are made using CMOS, the current is almost proportional to the clock speed, the CPU drawing almost no current between clock cycles. *(Refer to Page 44, Chapter 5)*

E

ESD (ElectroStatic Discharge)   an antistatic wrist strap, ESD wrist strap, or ground bracelet is an antistatic device used to prevent electrostatic discharge (ESD) by safely grounding a person working on electronic equipment. *(Refer to page 26, Chapter 3)*

F

Floppy A: Drive   A device that allows your computer to read floppy disks. *(Refer to Page 11, Chapter 1)*

G

Gigabyte(s)   are a multiple of the unit byte for digital information storage. 1 *gigabyte* is 1000000000bytes. *(Refer to Page 10, Chapter 1)*

Gigahertz   *GHz (Gigahertz)* One billion cycles per second. *(Refer to Page 10, Chapter 1)*

H

Hard Drive   A disk drive that reads data stored on hard disks. Also called hard disk drive. *(Refer to Page 69, Chapter 5)*

I

IDE (**I**ntegrated **D**rive **E**lectronics) is a standard electronic interface used between a computer motherboard's data paths or bus and the computer's disk storage devices. *(Refer to Page 70, Chapter 5)*

IDE Cable A 40-pin ribbon cable for CD-ROMs and similar devices such as hard drives, and DVD-Rom drives. *(Refer to Page 78, Chapter 5)*

Internet A vast computer network linking smaller computer networks worldwide (usually preceded by the). The Internet includes commercial, educational, governmental, and other networks, all of which use the same set of communications protocols. *(Refer to Page 9, Chapter 1)*

Intel Processors A *CPU* chip manufactured by Intel. *(Refer to Page 10, Chapter 1)*

I/O Plate Is a metal shield that slips on the I/O Ports of the motherboard to protect it from dust and dirt. *(Refer to Page 39, Chapter 5)*

I/O Ports (**I**nput/**O**utput port) A pathway into and out of the computer. *(Refer to Page 79, Chapter 5)*

J

Jumper Is a short length of conductor used to close a break in or bypass part of an electrical circuit. *(Refer to Page 43, 119, Chapter 5)*

K

Keyboard and Mouse   The primary input devices used with a computer. *(Refer to Page 11, Chapter 1)*

M

Memory   The most common type is DDR, and *RAM,* but in the general sense it can be any device that can hold data in machine-readable format. *(Refer to Page 11, 54, Chapter 1)*

Monitor   A device that displays signals on a computer screen. *(Refer to Page 11, Chapter 1)*

Motherboard   The main board of a computer, usually containing the circuitry for the central processing unit, keyboard, and monitor. *(Refer to Page 11, Chapter 1)*

N

NTFS   (**N**ew **T**echnology **F**ile **S**ystem) is the standard file system of Windows NT, including its later versions Windows 2000, Windows XP, Windows Server 2003, Windows Server 2008, Windows Vista, and Windows 7. *(Refer to Page 85, Chapter 6)*

P

PCI (**P**eripheral **C**omponent **I**nterconnect) A standard for connecting computers and their peripherals. *(Refer to Page 63, Chapter 5)*

Pin 1 A terminal on a through-hole component. *(Refer to Page 76, Chapter 5)*

Power Supply A power supply is a device that supplies electrical energy to one or more electric loads. *(Refer to Page 11, 42, Chapters 1, 5)*

Processor Microchip implanted in a CPU's hard drive that processes instructions sent to it by the computer and software programs. *(Refer to Page 50, Chapter 5)*

S

SATA Serial ATA (SATA or **S**erial **A**dvanced **T**echnology **A**ttachment) is a computer bus interface for connecting host bus adapters to mass storage devices. *(Refer to Page 76, Chapter 5)*

Sockets Adapters for using socket processors in bus-compatible slot motherboards. *(Refer to Page 15, 121 Chapter 2)*

T

Thermal Grease A viscous material (such as silicone grease) that is applied between two surfaces to enhance heat transfer between them. *(Refer to Page 51, Chapter 5)*

Tower Case An improvement to the standard desktop case, a tower case is flipped 90 degrees to accommodate more inside and to make it more convenient by allowing the case to be placed on the floor instead of on the desk. *(Refer to Page 11, Chapter 1)*

U

USB Universal Serial Bus, a connection technology for attaching peripheral devices to a computer, providing fast data exchange.
 (Refer to Page 61, Chapter 5)

USB Port(s) Is a specification to establish communication between devices and a host controller. *(Refer to Page 61, Chapter 5)*

V

Video Card (Graphics Card) An important device inside a computer or gaming console. This card displays graphics to your monitor or TV. *(Refer to Page 11, Chapter 1)*

Picture Diagrams:

Motherboard

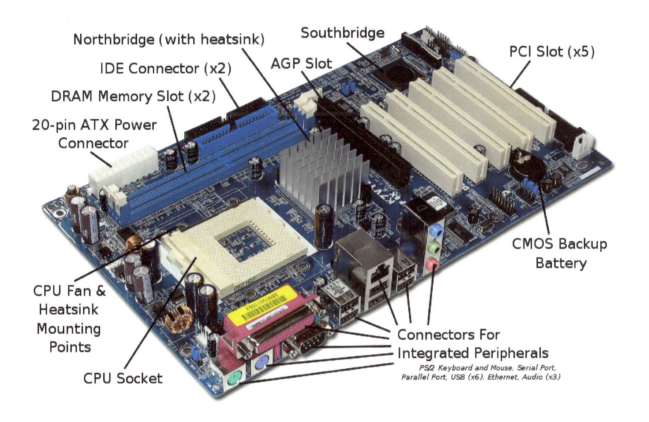

Northbridge (with heatsink)

Southbridge

PCI Slot (x5)

IDE Connector (x2)

AGP Slot

DRAM Memory Slot (x2)

20-pin ATX Power Connector

CMOS Backup Battery

CPU Fan & Heatsink Mounting Points

Connectors For Integrated Peripherals

CPU Socket

PS/2 Keyboard and Mouse, Serial Port, Parallel Port, USB (x6), Ethernet, Audio (x3)

Motherboard Specs:

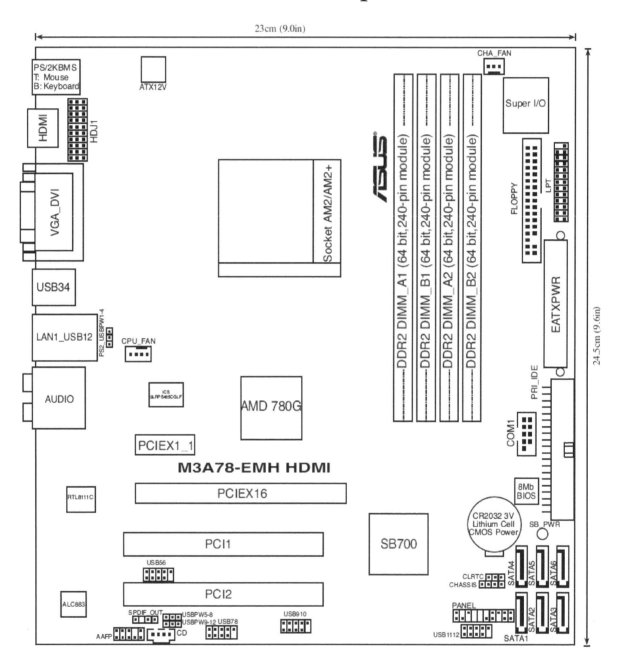

IDE Cables Connecting to Motherboard:

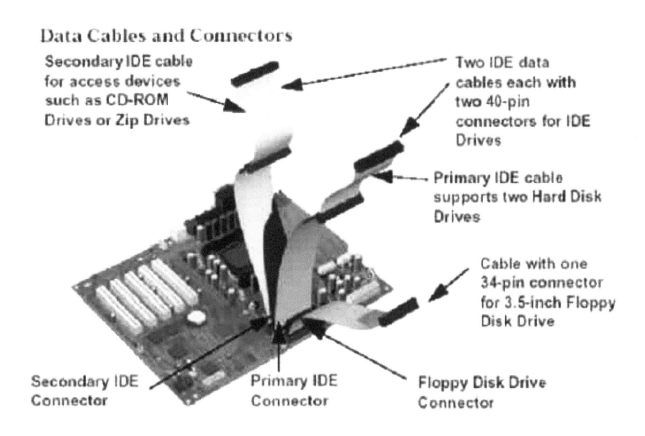

Data Cables and Connectors

Secondary IDE cable for access devices such as CD-ROM Drives or Zip Drives

Two IDE data cables each with two 40-pin connectors for IDE Drives

Primary IDE cable supports two Hard Disk Drives

Cable with one 34-pin connector for 3.5-inch Floppy Disk Drive

Secondary IDE Connector

Primary IDE Connector

Floppy Disk Drive Connector

Jumper Specifications:

Options jumper block

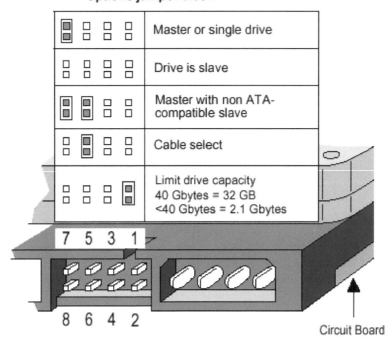

| | | Master or single drive |
| Drive is slave |
| Master with non ATA-compatible slave |
| Cable select |
| Limit drive capacity
40 Gbytes = 32 GB
<40 Gbytes = 2.1 Gbytes |

7 5 3 1

8 6 4 2

Circuit Board

I/O Ports:

PS/2 Keyboard Port

S/PDIF Ports

Serial ATA Port

USB 2.0 Ports

Center/Subwoofer

Side Speakers

Microphone
Line-Out
Wi-Fi Antenna In

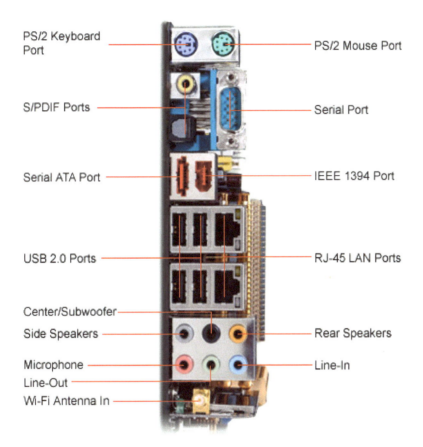

PS/2 Mouse Port

Serial Port

IEEE 1394 Port

RJ-45 LAN Ports

Rear Speakers

Line-In

List of CPU Sockets:

Socket 1- 80486

Socket 2- 80486

Socket 3- 80486 (3.3 V and 5 V) and compatibles

Socket 4-Intel Pentium 60/66 MHz

Socket 5- Intel Pentium 75-133 MHz; AMD K5;IDT Win Chip C6, Win Chip 2

Socket 6- 80486

Socket 7- Intel Pentium, Pentium MMX; AMD K6

Super Socket 7 -AMD K6-2, AMD K6-III; Rise mP6

Socket 8- Intel Pentium Pro

Socket 370- Intel Pentium III, Celeron; Cyrix III;VIA C3

Socket 423- Intel Pentium 4

Socket 463(also known as Socket NexGen) - NexGen Nx586

Socket 478- Intel Pentium 4, Celeron, Pentium 4 Extreme Edition

Socket 479- Intel Pentium M, Celeron M, Core Duo, & Core Solo

Socket 486- 80486

Socket 499- DEC Alpha 21164a

Socket 563- AMD low-power mobile Athlon XP-M (μ-PGA Socket, mostly mobile parts)

Socket 603- Intel Xeon

Socket 604- Intel Xeon

Socket 754- AMD single-processor systems using single-channel DDR-SDRAM, including AMD Athlon 64,Sempron, Turion 64 LGA 771 (also known as Socket 771) - Intel Xeon LGA 775 (also known as Socket 775 or Socket T) - Intel Pentium 4,Pentium D, Celeron D, Pentium Extreme Edition, Core 2 Duo, Core 2 Extreme, Celeron

Socket 939- AMD single-processor systems using dual-channel DDR-SDRAM, including Athlon 64,Athlon 64 FX to 1 GHz, Athlon 64 X2, Opteron100-series Socket 940- AMD single and multi-processor systems using DDR-SDRAM, including AMD Opteron , Athlon 64 FX

Socket A (also known as Socket 462) -
AMD Athlon, Duron, Athlon XP, Athlon XP-M, Athlon MP, and Sempron

Socket F (also known as Socket 1207) - AMD multi-processor systems using DDR2-SDRAM, including AMD

Opteron, replaces Socket 940

Socket AM2- AMD single-processor systems using DDR2-SDRAM, replaces Socket 754 and Socket939

Socket AM2+- Future AMD Socket for single processor systems, support DDR2 and HyperTransport3 with separated power lanes. Planned for mid 2007 to Q3 2007, replaces Socket AM2 (PGA 940 contacts)

CPU Slots:

Slot 1- Intel Celeron, Pentium II, Pentium III

Slot 2- Intel Pentium II Xeon, Pentium III Xeon

Slot A- AMD Athlon

Slot B - DEC Alpha

REFERENCES

www.answers.com

www.wikipedia.com

About The Author

John Gower III was born in Philadelphia, Pennsylvania in 1985, where he grew up in the town of Broadheadsville raised by his mother and father. John attended Bangor Area High School, graduating in 2003. John attended college at Information Computer Systems Institute in Allentown, Pennsylvania, where he graduated with an associate's degree in Business/Data Networking in 2005. John now has ten years experience in computers working with software, hardware, networking, and web design.

John has professional knowledge and skills in; Windows 98 ®, Windows 2000 ®, Windows 2000, Advanced Server ®, Windows XP Home Edition ®, Windows XP Pro ®, Windows Vista ®, Windows 7 ® , Linux ®, Front Page 2002®, Dreamweaver® , Microsoft Access 2000® , Microsoft Word 2000®, Microsoft Excel 2000®, Microsoft PowerPoint 2000®, DOS®, Web Design®.

John also has numerous certifications in the field of computers. John started writing books later on in his life. He published his first book on July 1, 2011 called, "How to Build a Computer (For Beginners)"©. John is currently still writing and publishing more educational books for schools, colleges and people all around the world. John aims to educate readers about the knowledge of technology geared to people who are interested in learning, and who are not familiar with computers.

To know more about this book and details on how to purchase a copy or if you are a store looking to purchase this book in a bulk order please visit my website at http://www.jghitech.com

Visit: http://www.jghitech.com

If you would like to purchase a shirt or coffee mug, please visit the gift shop on the author's website at;

http://www.jghitech.com and click on the Gift Shop link at the top of the page.